I0110623

KEEP IT SECRET

A Journal for Your Passwords

Activinotes

Activinotes

DAILY JOURNALS, PLANNERS, NOTEBOOKS AND OTHER BLANK BOOKS

All Rights reserved. No part of this book may be reproduced or used in any way or form or by any means whether electronic or mechanical, this means that you cannot record or photocopy any material ideas or tips that are provided in this book.

Copyright 2016

Password Journal

Account Name: _____

Website : _____

User I.D. : _____

Email Used : _____

Password : _____

Password Change	Date

Notes : _____
_____
_____
_____
_____

i ♥ *purple*

Notes : _____
_____
_____
_____

Account Name: _____

Website : _____

User I.D. : _____

Email Used : _____

Password : _____

Password Change	Date

Account Name: _____

Website : _____

User I.D. : _____

Email Used : _____

Password : _____

Password Change	Date

i ♥ *purple*

Notes : _____
_____
_____
_____

Password Journal

Account Name: _____

Website : _____

User I.D. : _____

Email Used : _____

Password : _____

Password Change	Date

Notes :
_____
_____
_____
_____

Account Name: _____

Website : _____

User I.D. : _____

Email Used : _____

Password : _____

Password Change	Date

Notes :
_____
_____
_____
_____

Account Name: _____

Website : _____

User I.D. : _____

Email Used : _____

Password : _____

Password Change	Date

Notes :
_____
_____
_____
_____

Password Journal

Account Name: _____
Website : _____
User I.D. : _____
Email Used : _____
Password : _____

Password Change	Date

Notes :
_____
_____
_____
_____

i PURPLE

Notes :
_____
_____
_____
_____

Account Name: _____
Website : _____
User I.D. : _____
Email Used : _____
Password : _____

Password Change	Date

Account Name: _____
Website : _____
User I.D. : _____
Email Used : _____
Password : _____

Password Change	Date

i PURPLE

Notes :
_____
_____
_____
_____

Password Journal

Account Name: _____

Website : _____

User I.D. : _____

Email Used : _____

Password : _____

Password Change	Date

Notes :
_____
_____
_____
_____
_____

Account Name: _____

Website : _____

User I.D. : _____

Email Used : _____

Password : _____

Password Change	Date

Notes :
_____
_____
_____
_____

Account Name: _____

Website : _____

User I.D. : _____

Email Used : _____

Password : _____

Password Change	Date

Notes :
_____
_____
_____
_____

Password Journal

Account Name: _____

Website : _____

User I.D. : _____

Email Used : _____

Password : _____

Password Change	Date

Notes :
_____
_____
_____
_____

Account Name: _____

Website : _____

User I.D. : _____

Email Used : _____

Password : _____

Password Change	Date

Notes :
_____
_____
_____
_____

Account Name: _____

Website : _____

User I.D. : _____

Email Used : _____

Password : _____

Password Change	Date

Notes :
_____
_____
_____
_____

Password Journal

Notes

Password Journal

Account Name: _____

Website : _____

User I.D. : _____

Email Used : _____

Password : _____

Password Change	Date

Notes :
_____
_____
_____
_____

i ♥ PuRPle

Notes :
_____
_____
_____
_____

Account Name: _____

Website : _____

User I.D. : _____

Email Used : _____

Password : _____

Password Change	Date

Account Name: _____

Website : _____

User I.D. : _____

Email Used : _____

Password : _____

Password Change	Date

i ♥ PuRPle

Notes :
_____
_____
_____
_____

Password Journal

Account Name: _____

Website : _____

User I.D. : _____

Email Used : _____

Password : _____

Password Change	Date

Notes :

_____

_____

_____

_____

Account Name: _____

Website : _____

User I.D. : _____

Email Used : _____

Password : _____

Password Change	Date

Notes :

_____

_____

_____

_____

Account Name: _____

Website : _____

User I.D. : _____

Email Used : _____

Password : _____

Password Change	Date

Notes :

_____

_____

_____

_____

Password Journal

Account Name: _____

Website : _____

User I.D. : _____

Email Used : _____

Password : _____

Password Change	Date

Notes :
_____
_____
_____
_____

Account Name: _____

Website : _____

User I.D. : _____

Email Used : _____

Password : _____

Password Change	Date

Notes :
_____
_____
_____
_____

Account Name: _____

Website : _____

User I.D. : _____

Email Used : _____

Password : _____

Password Change	Date

Notes :
_____
_____
_____
_____

Password Journal

Account Name: _____

Website : _____

User I.D. : _____

Email Used : _____

Password : _____

Password Change	Date

Notes :

_____

_____

_____

_____

Notes :

_____

_____

_____

_____

Account Name: _____

Website : _____

User I.D. : _____

Email Used : _____

Password : _____

Password Change	Date

Account Name: _____

Website : _____

User I.D. : _____

Email Used : _____

Password : _____

Password Change	Date

Notes :

_____

_____

_____

_____

Password Journal

Account Name: _____

Website : _____

User I.D. : _____

Email Used : _____

Password : _____

Password Change	Date

Notes :
_____
_____
_____
_____

i ❤ Purple

Notes :
_____
_____
_____
_____

Account Name: _____

Website : _____

User I.D. : _____

Email Used : _____

Password : _____

Password Change	Date

Account Name: _____

Website : _____

User I.D. : _____

Email Used : _____

Password : _____

Password Change	Date

i ❤ Purple

Notes :
_____
_____
_____
_____

Password Journal

Notes

Password Journal

Account Name: _____

Website : _____

User I.D. : _____

Email Used : _____

Password : _____

Password Change	Date

Notes :
_____
_____
_____
_____

Notes :
_____
_____
_____
_____

Account Name: _____

Website : _____

User I.D. : _____

Email Used : _____

Password : _____

Password Change	Date

Account Name: _____

Website : _____

User I.D. : _____

Email Used : _____

Password : _____

Password Change	Date

Notes :
_____
_____
_____
_____

Password Journal

Account Name: _____

Website : _____

User I.D. : _____

Email Used : _____

Password : _____

Password Change	Date

Notes :

_____

_____

_____

_____

Account Name: _____

Website : _____

User I.D. : _____

Email Used : _____

Password : _____

Password Change	Date

Notes :

_____

_____

_____

_____

Account Name: _____

Website : _____

User I.D. : _____

Email Used : _____

Password : _____

Password Change	Date

Notes :

_____

_____

_____

_____

Password Journal

Account Name: _____

Website : _____

User I.D. : _____

Email Used : _____

Password : _____

Password Change	Date

Notes :
_____
_____
_____
_____

i ♥ purple

Notes :
_____
_____
_____
_____

Account Name: _____

Website : _____

User I.D. : _____

Email Used : _____

Password : _____

Password Change	Date

i ♥ purple

Account Name: _____

Website : _____

User I.D. : _____

Email Used : _____

Password : _____

Password Change	Date

Notes :
_____
_____
_____
_____

Password Journal

Account Name: _____

Website : _____

User I.D. : _____

Email Used : _____

Password : _____

Password Change	Date

Notes :
_____
_____
_____
_____

Account Name: _____

Website : _____

User I.D. : _____

Email Used : _____

Password : _____

Password Change	Date

Notes :
_____
_____
_____
_____

Account Name: _____

Website : _____

User I.D. : _____

Email Used : _____

Password : _____

Password Change	Date

Notes :
_____
_____
_____
_____

Password Journal

Account Name: _____

Website : _____

User I.D. : _____

Email Used : _____

Password : _____

Password Change	Date

Notes :
_____
_____
_____
_____

Account Name: _____

Website : _____

User I.D. : _____

Email Used : _____

Password : _____

Password Change	Date

Notes :
_____
_____
_____
_____

Account Name: _____

Website : _____

User I.D. : _____

Email Used : _____

Password : _____

Password Change	Date

Notes :
_____
_____
_____
_____

Password Journal

Notes

Password Journal

Account Name: _____

Website : _____

User I.D. : _____

Email Used : _____

Password : _____

Password Change	Date

Notes :
_____
_____
_____
_____

i
PUrPle

Account Name: _____

Website : _____

User I.D. : _____

Email Used : _____

Password : _____

Password Change	Date

Notes :
_____
_____
_____
_____

Account Name: _____

Website : _____

User I.D. : _____

Email Used : _____

Password : _____

Password Change	Date

i
PUrPle

Notes :
_____
_____
_____
_____

Password Journal

Account Name: _____

Website : _____

User I.D. : _____

Email Used : _____

Password : _____

Password Change	Date

Notes :
_____
_____
_____
_____

Account Name: _____

Website : _____

User I.D. : _____

Email Used : _____

Password : _____

Password Change	Date

Notes :
_____
_____
_____
_____

Account Name: _____

Website : _____

User I.D. : _____

Email Used : _____

Password : _____

Password Change	Date

Notes :
_____
_____
_____
_____

Password Journal

Account Name: _____

Website : _____

User I.D. : _____

Email Used : _____

Password : _____

Password Change	Date

Notes :

_____

_____

_____

_____

Account Name: _____

Website : _____

User I.D. : _____

Email Used : _____

Password : _____

Password Change	Date

Notes :

_____

_____

_____

_____

Account Name: _____

Website : _____

User I.D. : _____

Email Used : _____

Password : _____

Password Change	Date

Notes :

_____

_____

_____

_____

Password Journal

Account Name: _____

Website : _____

User I.D. : _____

Email Used : _____

Password : _____

Password Change	Date

Notes :

_____

_____

_____

_____

Account Name: _____

Website : _____

User I.D. : _____

Email Used : _____

Password : _____

Password Change	Date

Notes :

_____

_____

_____

_____

Account Name: _____

Website : _____

User I.D. : _____

Email Used : _____

Password : _____

Password Change	Date

Notes :

_____

_____

_____

_____

Password Journal

Account Name: _____

Website : _____

User I.D. : _____

Email Used : _____

Password : _____

Password Change	Date

Notes :

_____

_____

_____

_____

i ♥ purple

Notes :

_____

_____

_____

_____

Account Name: _____

Website : _____

User I.D. : _____

Email Used : _____

Password : _____

Password Change	Date

Account Name: _____

Website : _____

User I.D. : _____

Email Used : _____

Password : _____

Password Change	Date

i ♥ purple

Notes :

_____

_____

_____

_____

Password Journal

Notes

Password Journal

Account Name: _____

Website : _____

User I.D. : _____

Email Used : _____

Password : _____

Password Change	Date

Notes :

_____

_____

_____

_____

Notes :

_____

_____

_____

_____

Account Name: _____

Website : _____

User I.D. : _____

Email Used : _____

Password : _____

Password Change	Date

Account Name: _____

Website : _____

User I.D. : _____

Email Used : _____

Password : _____

Password Change	Date

Notes :

_____

_____

_____

_____

Password Journal

Account Name: _____

Website : _____

User I.D. : _____

Email Used : _____

Password : _____

Password Change	Date

Notes :
_____
_____
_____
_____

Account Name: _____

Website : _____

User I.D. : _____

Email Used : _____

Password : _____

Password Change	Date

Notes :
_____
_____
_____
_____

Account Name: _____

Website : _____

User I.D. : _____

Email Used : _____

Password : _____

Password Change	Date

Notes :
_____
_____
_____
_____

Password Journal

Account Name: _____

Website : _____

User I.D. : _____

Email Used : _____

Password : _____

Password Change	Date

Notes :
_____
_____
_____
_____

Account Name: _____

Website : _____

User I.D. : _____

Email Used : _____

Password : _____

Password Change	Date

Notes :
_____
_____
_____
_____

Account Name: _____

Website : _____

User I.D. : _____

Email Used : _____

Password : _____

Password Change	Date

Notes :
_____
_____
_____
_____

Password Journal

Account Name: _____

Website : _____

User I.D. : _____

Email Used : _____

Password : _____

Password Change	Date

Notes :
_____
_____
_____
_____
_____

Account Name: _____

Website : _____

User I.D. : _____

Email Used : _____

Password : _____

Password Change	Date

Notes :
_____
_____
_____
_____

Account Name: _____

Website : _____

User I.D. : _____

Email Used : _____

Password : _____

Password Change	Date

Notes :
_____
_____
_____
_____

Password Journal

Account Name: _____

Website : _____

User I.D. : _____

Email Used : _____

Password : _____

Password Change	Date

Notes :
_____
_____
_____
_____

Notes :
_____
_____
_____
_____

Account Name: _____

Website : _____

User I.D. : _____

Email Used : _____

Password : _____

Password Change	Date

Account Name: _____

Website : _____

User I.D. : _____

Email Used : _____

Password : _____

Password Change	Date

Notes :
_____
_____
_____

Password Journal

Notes

Password Journal

Account Name: _____

Website : _____

User I.D. : _____

Email Used : _____

Password : _____

Password Change	Date

Notes :
_____
_____
_____
_____

i ♡ PURPLE

Account Name: _____

Website : _____

User I.D. : _____

Email Used : _____

Password : _____

Password Change	Date

Notes :
_____
_____
_____
_____

Account Name: _____

Website : _____

User I.D. : _____

Email Used : _____

Password : _____

Password Change	Date

i ♡ PURPLE

Notes :
_____
_____
_____
_____

Password Journal

Account Name: _____

Website : _____

User I.D. : _____

Email Used : _____

Password : _____

Password Change	Date

Notes :

_____

_____

_____

_____

Notes :

_____

_____

_____

_____

Account Name: _____

Website : _____

User I.D. : _____

Email Used : _____

Password : _____

Password Change	Date

Account Name: _____

Website : _____

User I.D. : _____

Email Used : _____

Password : _____

Password Change	Date

Notes :

_____

_____

_____

_____

Password Journal

Account Name: _____

Website : _____

User I.D. : _____

Email Used : _____

Password : _____

Password Change	Date

Notes :
_____
_____
_____
_____

i ♥ purple

Account Name: _____

Website : _____

User I.D. : _____

Email Used : _____

Password : _____

Password Change	Date

Notes :
_____
_____
_____
_____

Account Name: _____

Website : _____

User I.D. : _____

Email Used : _____

Password : _____

Password Change	Date

i ♥ purple

Notes :
_____
_____
_____
_____

Password Journal

Account Name: _____

Website : _____

User I.D. : _____

Email Used : _____

Password : _____

Password Change	Date

Notes :
_____
_____
_____
_____

Notes :
_____
_____
_____
_____

Account Name: _____

Website : _____

User I.D. : _____

Email Used : _____

Password : _____

Password Change	Date

Account Name: _____

Website : _____

User I.D. : _____

Email Used : _____

Password : _____

Password Change	Date

Notes :
_____
_____
_____
_____

Password Journal

Account Name: _____

Website : _____

User I.D. : _____

Email Used : _____

Password : _____

Password Change	Date

Notes :
_____
_____
_____
_____

Account Name: _____

Website : _____

User I.D. : _____

Email Used : _____

Password : _____

Password Change	Date

Notes :
_____
_____
_____
_____

Account Name: _____

Website : _____

User I.D. : _____

Email Used : _____

Password : _____

Password Change	Date

Notes :
_____
_____
_____

Password Journal

Notes

Password Journal

Account Name: _____

Website : _____

User I.D. : _____

Email Used : _____

Password : _____

Password Change	Date

Notes :
_____
_____
_____
_____

i ♥ purple

Notes :
_____
_____
_____
_____

Account Name: _____

Website : _____

User I.D. : _____

Email Used : _____

Password : _____

Password Change	Date

Account Name: _____

Website : _____

User I.D. : _____

Email Used : _____

Password : _____

Password Change	Date

i ♥ purple

Notes :
_____
_____
_____
_____

Password Journal

Account Name: _____

Website : _____

User I.D. : _____

Email Used : _____

Password : _____

Password Change	Date

Notes :
_____
_____
_____
_____

i ♡ Purple

Account Name: _____

Website : _____

User I.D. : _____

Email Used : _____

Password : _____

Password Change	Date

Notes :
_____
_____
_____
_____

Account Name: _____

Website : _____

User I.D. : _____

Email Used : _____

Password : _____

Password Change	Date

i ♡ Purple

Notes :
_____
_____
_____
_____

Password Journal

Account Name: _____

Website : _____

User I.D. : _____

Email Used : _____

Password : _____

Password Change	Date

Notes :

_____

_____

_____

_____

i PURPLE

Account Name: _____

Website : _____

User I.D. : _____

Email Used : _____

Password : _____

Password Change	Date

Notes :

_____

_____

_____

_____

Account Name: _____

Website : _____

User I.D. : _____

Email Used : _____

Password : _____

Password Change	Date

i PURPLE

Notes :

_____

_____

_____

_____

Password Journal

Account Name: _____

Website : _____

User I.D. : _____

Email Used : _____

Password : _____

Password Change	Date

Notes :
_____
_____
_____
_____

Account Name: _____

Website : _____

User I.D. : _____

Email Used : _____

Password : _____

Password Change	Date

Notes :
_____
_____
_____
_____

Account Name: _____

Website : _____

User I.D. : _____

Email Used : _____

Password : _____

Password Change	Date

Notes :
_____
_____
_____
_____

Password Journal

Account Name: _____

Website : _____

User I.D. : _____

Email Used : _____

Password : _____

Password Change	Date

Notes : _____
_____
_____
_____

Account Name: _____

Website : _____

User I.D. : _____

Email Used : _____

Password : _____

Password Change	Date

Notes : _____
_____
_____
_____

Account Name: _____

Website : _____

User I.D. : _____

Email Used : _____

Password : _____

Password Change	Date

Notes : _____
_____
_____
_____

Password Journal

Notes

Password Journal

Account Name: _____

Website : _____

User I.D. : _____

Email Used : _____

Password : _____

Password Change	Date

Notes :
_____
_____
_____
_____

i ♥ PURPLE

Account Name: _____

Website : _____

User I.D. : _____

Email Used : _____

Password : _____

Password Change	Date

Notes :
_____
_____
_____
_____

Account Name: _____

Website : _____

User I.D. : _____

Email Used : _____

Password : _____

Password Change	Date

i ♥ PURPLE

Notes :
_____
_____
_____
_____

Password Journal

Account Name: _____

Website : _____

User I.D. : _____

Email Used : _____

Password : _____

Password Change	Date

Notes :

_____

_____

_____

_____

Account Name: _____

Website : _____

User I.D. : _____

Email Used : _____

Password : _____

Password Change	Date

Notes :

_____

_____

_____

_____

Account Name: _____

Website : _____

User I.D. : _____

Email Used : _____

Password : _____

Password Change	Date

Notes :

_____

_____

_____

_____

Password Journal

Account Name: _____

Website : _____

User I.D. : _____

Email Used : _____

Password : _____

Password Change	Date

Notes :

_____

_____

_____

_____

Account Name: _____

Website : _____

User I.D. : _____

Email Used : _____

Password : _____

Password Change	Date

Notes :

_____

_____

_____

_____

Account Name: _____

Website : _____

User I.D. : _____

Email Used : _____

Password : _____

Password Change	Date

Notes :

_____

_____

_____

_____

Password Journal

Account Name: _____

Website : _____

User I.D. : _____

Email Used : _____

Password : _____

Password Change	Date

Notes :
_____
_____
_____
_____

Account Name: _____

Website : _____

User I.D. : _____

Email Used : _____

Password : _____

Password Change	Date

Notes :
_____
_____
_____
_____

Account Name: _____

Website : _____

User I.D. : _____

Email Used : _____

Password : _____

Password Change	Date

Notes :
_____
_____
_____
_____

Password Journal

Account Name: _____

Website : _____

User I.D. : _____

Email Used : _____

Password : _____

Password Change	Date

Notes : _____
_____
_____
_____

Account Name: _____

Website : _____

User I.D. : _____

Email Used : _____

Password : _____

Password Change	Date

Notes : _____
_____
_____
_____

Account Name: _____

Website : _____

User I.D. : _____

Email Used : _____

Password : _____

Password Change	Date

Notes : _____
_____
_____
_____

Password Journal

Notes

Password Journal

Account Name: _____

Website : _____

User I.D. : _____

Email Used : _____

Password : _____

Password Change	Date

Notes :
_____
_____
_____
_____
_____

Account Name: _____

Website : _____

User I.D. : _____

Email Used : _____

Password : _____

Password Change	Date

Notes :
_____
_____
_____
_____

Account Name: _____

Website : _____

User I.D. : _____

Email Used : _____

Password : _____

Password Change	Date

Notes :
_____
_____
_____
_____

Password Journal

Account Name: _____

Website : _____

User I.D. : _____

Email Used : _____

Password : _____

Password Change	Date

Notes :
_____
_____
_____
_____

Notes :
_____
_____
_____
_____

Account Name: _____

Website : _____

User I.D. : _____

Email Used : _____

Password : _____

Password Change	Date

Account Name: _____

Website : _____

User I.D. : _____

Email Used : _____

Password : _____

Password Change	Date

Notes :
_____
_____
_____
_____

Password Journal

Account Name: _____

Website : _____

User I.D. : _____

Email Used : _____

Password : _____

Password Change	Date

Notes : _____
_____
_____
_____

i ♡♡ Purple

Notes : _____
_____
_____
_____

Account Name: _____

Website : _____

User I.D. : _____

Email Used : _____

Password : _____

Password Change	Date

Account Name: _____

Website : _____

User I.D. : _____

Email Used : _____

Password : _____

Password Change	Date

i ♡♡ Purple

Notes : _____
_____
_____
_____

Password Journal

Account Name: _____

Website : _____

User I.D. : _____

Email Used : _____

Password : _____

Password Change	Date

Notes :
_____
_____
_____
_____

Account Name: _____

Website : _____

User I.D. : _____

Email Used : _____

Password : _____

Password Change	Date

Notes :
_____
_____
_____
_____

Account Name: _____

Website : _____

User I.D. : _____

Email Used : _____

Password : _____

Password Change	Date

Notes :
_____
_____
_____
_____

Password Journal

Account Name: _____

Website : _____

User I.D. : _____

Email Used : _____

Password : _____

Password Change	Date

Notes : _____
_____
_____
_____
_____

i ♥ purple

Notes : _____
_____
_____
_____
_____

Account Name: _____

Website : _____

User I.D. : _____

Email Used : _____

Password : _____

Password Change	Date

i ♥ purple

Account Name: _____

Website : _____

User I.D. : _____

Email Used : _____

Password : _____

Password Change	Date

Notes : _____
_____
_____
_____

Password Journal

Notes

Password Journal

Account Name: _____

Website : _____

User I.D. : _____

Email Used : _____

Password : _____

Password Change	Date

Notes :
_____
_____
_____
_____

Notes :
_____
_____
_____
_____

Account Name: _____

Website : _____

User I.D. : _____

Email Used : _____

Password : _____

Password Change	Date

Account Name: _____

Website : _____

User I.D. : _____

Email Used : _____

Password : _____

Password Change	Date

Notes :
_____
_____
_____
_____

Password Journal

Account Name: _____

Website : _____

User I.D. : _____

Email Used : _____

Password : _____

Password Change	Date

Notes :

_____

_____

_____

_____

Notes :

_____

_____

_____

_____

Account Name: _____

Website : _____

User I.D. : _____

Email Used : _____

Password : _____

Password Change	Date

Account Name: _____

Website : _____

User I.D. : _____

Email Used : _____

Password : _____

Password Change	Date

Notes :

_____

_____

_____

_____

Password Journal

Account Name: _____

Website : _____

User I.D. : _____

Email Used : _____

Password : _____

Password Change	Date

Notes :
_____
_____
_____
_____

i ♥ purple

Notes :
_____
_____
_____
_____

Account Name: _____

Website : _____

User I.D. : _____

Email Used : _____

Password : _____

Password Change	Date

i ♥ purple

Account Name: _____

Website : _____

User I.D. : _____

Email Used : _____

Password : _____

Password Change	Date

Notes :
_____
_____
_____
_____

Password Journal

Account Name: _____

Website : _____

User I.D. : _____

Email Used : _____

Password : _____

Password Change	Date

Notes :
_____
_____
_____
_____

Account Name: _____

Website : _____

User I.D. : _____

Email Used : _____

Password : _____

Password Change	Date

Notes :
_____
_____
_____
_____

Account Name: _____

Website : _____

User I.D. : _____

Email Used : _____

Password : _____

Password Change	Date

Notes :
_____
_____
_____
_____

Password Journal

Account Name: _____

Website : _____

User I.D. : _____

Email Used : _____

Password : _____

Password Change	Date

Notes :
_____
_____
_____
_____

i ♥ Purple

Account Name: _____

Website : _____

User I.D. : _____

Email Used : _____

Password : _____

Password Change	Date

Notes :
_____
_____
_____
_____

Account Name: _____

Website : _____

User I.D. : _____

Email Used : _____

Password : _____

Password Change	Date

i ♥ Purple

Notes :
_____
_____
_____
_____

Password Journal

Notes

Password Journal

Account Name: _____

Website : _____

User I.D. : _____

Email Used : _____

Password : _____

Password Change	Date

Notes : _____
_____
_____
_____

Account Name: _____

Website : _____

User I.D. : _____

Email Used : _____

Password : _____

Password Change	Date

Notes : _____
_____
_____
_____

Account Name: _____

Website : _____

User I.D. : _____

Email Used : _____

Password : _____

Password Change	Date

Notes : _____
_____
_____
_____

Password Journal

Account Name: _____

Website : _____

User I.D. : _____

Email Used : _____

Password : _____

Password Change	Date

Notes :

_____

_____

_____

_____

Account Name: _____

Website : _____

User I.D. : _____

Email Used : _____

Password : _____

Password Change	Date

Notes :

_____

_____

_____

_____

Account Name: _____

Website : _____

User I.D. : _____

Email Used : _____

Password : _____

Password Change	Date

Notes :

_____

_____

_____

_____

Password Journal

Account Name: _____

Website : _____

User I.D. : _____

Email Used : _____

Password : _____

Password Change	Date

Notes :
_____
_____
_____
_____

i ♥ Purple

Account Name: _____

Website : _____

User I.D. : _____

Email Used : _____

Password : _____

Password Change	Date

Notes :
_____
_____
_____
_____

Account Name: _____

Website : _____

User I.D. : _____

Email Used : _____

Password : _____

Password Change	Date

i ♥ Purple

Notes :
_____
_____
_____

Password Journal

Account Name: _____

Website : _____

User I.D. : _____

Email Used : _____

Password : _____

Password Change	Date

Notes :
_____
_____
_____
_____

Account Name: _____

Website : _____

User I.D. : _____

Email Used : _____

Password : _____

Password Change	Date

Notes :
_____
_____
_____
_____

Account Name: _____

Website : _____

User I.D. : _____

Email Used : _____

Password : _____

Password Change	Date

Notes :
_____
_____
_____
_____

Password Journal

Account Name: _____

Website : _____

User I.D. : _____

Email Used : _____

Password : _____

Password Change	Date

Notes :
_____
_____
_____
_____

Notes :
_____
_____
_____
_____

Account Name: _____

Website : _____

User I.D. : _____

Email Used : _____

Password : _____

Password Change	Date

Account Name: _____

Website : _____

User I.D. : _____

Email Used : _____

Password : _____

Password Change	Date

Notes :
_____
_____
_____
_____

Password Journal

Notes

Password Journal

Account Name: _____

Website : _____

User I.D. : _____

Email Used : _____

Password : _____

Password Change	Date

Notes :
_____
_____
_____
_____

i ♥ PURPle

Notes :
_____
_____
_____
_____

Account Name: _____

Website : _____

User I.D. : _____

Email Used : _____

Password : _____

Password Change	Date

Account Name: _____

Website : _____

User I.D. : _____

Email Used : _____

Password : _____

Password Change	Date

i ♥ PURPle

Notes :
_____
_____
_____
_____

Password Journal

Account Name: _____

Website : _____

User I.D. : _____

Email Used : _____

Password : _____

Password Change	Date

Notes :
_____
_____
_____
_____

i ♡ Purple

Account Name: _____

Website : _____

User I.D. : _____

Email Used : _____

Password : _____

Password Change	Date

Notes :
_____
_____
_____
_____

Account Name: _____

Website : _____

User I.D. : _____

Email Used : _____

Password : _____

Password Change	Date

i ♡ Purple

Notes :
_____
_____
_____

Password Journal

Account Name: _____

Website : _____

User I.D. : _____

Email Used : _____

Password : _____

Password Change	Date

Notes :
_____
_____
_____
_____

i purple

Notes :
_____
_____
_____
_____

Account Name: _____

Website : _____

User I.D. : _____

Email Used : _____

Password : _____

Password Change	Date

i purple

Account Name: _____

Website : _____

User I.D. : _____

Email Used : _____

Password : _____

Password Change	Date

Notes :
_____
_____
_____
_____

Password Journal

Account Name: _____

Website : _____

User I.D. : _____

Email Used : _____

Password : _____

Password Change	Date

Notes :
_____
_____
_____
_____

Account Name: _____

Website : _____

User I.D. : _____

Email Used : _____

Password : _____

Password Change	Date

Notes :
_____
_____
_____
_____

Account Name: _____

Website : _____

User I.D. : _____

Email Used : _____

Password : _____

Password Change	Date

Notes :
_____
_____
_____
_____

Password Journal

Account Name: _____

Website : _____

User I.D. : _____

Email Used : _____

Password : _____

Password Change	Date

Notes :
_____
_____
_____
_____

i ♡ Purple

Notes :
_____
_____
_____
_____

Account Name: _____

Website : _____

User I.D. : _____

Email Used : _____

Password : _____

Password Change	Date

Account Name: _____

Website : _____

User I.D. : _____

Email Used : _____

Password : _____

Password Change	Date

i ♡ Purple

Notes :
_____
_____
_____

Password Journal

Notes

Password Journal

Account Name: _____

Website : _____

User I.D. : _____

Email Used : _____

Password : _____

Password Change	Date

Notes : _____
_____
_____
_____

Account Name: _____

Website : _____

User I.D. : _____

Email Used : _____

Password : _____

Password Change	Date

Notes : _____
_____
_____
_____

Account Name: _____

Website : _____

User I.D. : _____

Email Used : _____

Password : _____

Password Change	Date

Notes : _____
_____
_____
_____

Password Journal

Account Name: _____

Website : _____

User I.D. : _____

Email Used : _____

Password : _____

Password Change	Date

Notes :
_____
_____
_____
_____

Account Name: _____

Website : _____

User I.D. : _____

Email Used : _____

Password : _____

Password Change	Date

Notes :
_____
_____
_____
_____

Account Name: _____

Website : _____

User I.D. : _____

Email Used : _____

Password : _____

Password Change	Date

Notes :
_____
_____
_____
_____

Password Journal

Account Name: _____

Website : _____

User I.D. : _____

Email Used : _____

Password : _____

Password Change	Date

Notes :

_____
_____
_____
_____

i ♥ Purple

Account Name: _____

Website : _____

User I.D. : _____

Email Used : _____

Password : _____

Password Change	Date

Notes :

_____
_____
_____
_____

Account Name: _____

Website : _____

User I.D. : _____

Email Used : _____

Password : _____

Password Change	Date

i ♥ Purple

Notes :

_____
_____
_____
_____

Password Journal

Account Name: _____

Website : _____

User I.D. : _____

Email Used : _____

Password : _____

Password Change	Date

Notes : _____
_____
_____
_____
_____

Account Name: _____

Website : _____

User I.D. : _____

Email Used : _____

Password : _____

Password Change	Date

Notes : _____
_____
_____
_____

Account Name: _____

Website : _____

User I.D. : _____

Email Used : _____

Password : _____

Password Change	Date

Notes : _____
_____
_____
_____

Password Journal

Account Name: _____

Website : _____

User I.D. : _____

Email Used : _____

Password : _____

Password Change	Date

Notes :

_____

_____

_____

_____

Account Name: _____

Website : _____

User I.D. : _____

Email Used : _____

Password : _____

Password Change	Date

Notes :

_____

_____

_____

_____

Account Name: _____

Website : _____

User I.D. : _____

Email Used : _____

Password : _____

Password Change	Date

Notes :

_____

_____

Password Journal

Notes

Password Journal

Account Name: _____

Website : _____

User I.D. : _____

Email Used : _____

Password : _____

Password Change	Date

Notes :

_____

_____

_____

_____

Notes :

_____

_____

_____

_____

Account Name: _____

Website : _____

User I.D. : _____

Email Used : _____

Password : _____

Password Change	Date

Account Name: _____

Website : _____

User I.D. : _____

Email Used : _____

Password : _____

Password Change	Date

Notes :

_____

_____

_____

_____

Password Journal

Account Name: _____

Website : _____

User I.D. : _____

Email Used : _____

Password : _____

Password Change	Date

Notes :
_____
_____
_____
_____

Account Name: _____

Website : _____

User I.D. : _____

Email Used : _____

Password : _____

Password Change	Date

Notes :
_____
_____
_____
_____

Account Name: _____

Website : _____

User I.D. : _____

Email Used : _____

Password : _____

Password Change	Date

Notes :
_____
_____
_____

Password Journal

Account Name: _____

Website : _____

User I.D. : _____

Email Used : _____

Password : _____

Password Change	Date

Notes :

_____

_____

_____

_____

Account Name: _____

Website : _____

User I.D. : _____

Email Used : _____

Password : _____

Password Change	Date

Notes :

_____

_____

_____

_____

Account Name: _____

Website : _____

User I.D. : _____

Email Used : _____

Password : _____

Password Change	Date

Notes :

_____

_____

_____

Password Journal

Account Name: _____

Website : _____

User I.D. : _____

Email Used : _____

Password : _____

Password Change	Date

Notes :
_____
_____
_____
_____

Account Name: _____

Website : _____

User I.D. : _____

Email Used : _____

Password : _____

Password Change	Date

Notes :
_____
_____
_____
_____

Account Name: _____

Website : _____

User I.D. : _____

Email Used : _____

Password : _____

Password Change	Date

Notes :
_____
_____
_____
_____

Password Journal

Account Name: _____

Website : _____

User I.D. : _____

Email Used : _____

Password : _____

Password Change	Date

Notes : _____
_____
_____
_____

Account Name: _____

Website : _____

User I.D. : _____

Email Used : _____

Password : _____

Password Change	Date

Notes : _____
_____
_____
_____

Account Name: _____

Website : _____

User I.D. : _____

Email Used : _____

Password : _____

Password Change	Date

Notes : _____
_____
_____

Password Journal

Notes

Password Journal

Account Name: _____

Website : _____

User I.D. : _____

Email Used : _____

Password : _____

Password Change	Date

Notes :
_____
_____
_____
_____

Account Name: _____

Website : _____

User I.D. : _____

Email Used : _____

Password : _____

Password Change	Date

Notes :
_____
_____
_____
_____

Account Name: _____

Website : _____

User I.D. : _____

Email Used : _____

Password : _____

Password Change	Date

Notes :
_____
_____
_____
_____

Password Journal

Account Name: _____

Website : _____

User I.D. : _____

Email Used : _____

Password : _____

Password Change	Date

Notes :
_____
_____
_____
_____

i ♥ PURPLE

Notes :
_____
_____
_____
_____

Account Name: _____

Website : _____

User I.D. : _____

Email Used : _____

Password : _____

Password Change	Date

Account Name: _____

Website : _____

User I.D. : _____

Email Used : _____

Password : _____

Password Change	Date

i ♥ PURPLE

Notes :
_____
_____
_____
_____

Password Journal

Account Name: _____

Website : _____

User I.D. : _____

Email Used : _____

Password : _____

Password Change	Date

Notes :
_____
_____
_____
_____

i ♥ Purple

Notes :
_____
_____
_____
_____

Account Name: _____

Website : _____

User I.D. : _____

Email Used : _____

Password : _____

Password Change	Date

Account Name: _____

Website : _____

User I.D. : _____

Email Used : _____

Password : _____

Password Change	Date

i ♥ Purple

Notes :
_____
_____
_____
_____

Password Journal

Account Name: _____

Website : _____

User I.D. : _____

Email Used : _____

Password : _____

Password Change	Date

Notes :

_____

_____

_____

_____

Notes :

_____

_____

_____

_____

Account Name: _____

Website : _____

User I.D. : _____

Email Used : _____

Password : _____

Password Change	Date

Account Name: _____

Website : _____

User I.D. : _____

Email Used : _____

Password : _____

Password Change	Date

Notes :

_____

_____

_____

_____

Password Journal

Account Name: _____

Website : _____

User I.D. : _____

Email Used : _____

Password : _____

Password Change	Date

Notes :

_____

_____

_____

_____

Account Name: _____

Website : _____

User I.D. : _____

Email Used : _____

Password : _____

Password Change	Date

Notes :

_____

_____

_____

_____

Account Name: _____

Website : _____

User I.D. : _____

Email Used : _____

Password : _____

Password Change	Date

Notes :

_____

_____

_____

_____

Notes

Password Journal

Account Name: _____

Website : _____

User I.D. : _____

Email Used : _____

Password : _____

Password Change	Date

Notes :
_____
_____
_____
_____

Notes :
_____
_____
_____
_____

Account Name: _____

Website : _____

User I.D. : _____

Email Used : _____

Password : _____

Password Change	Date

Account Name: _____

Website : _____

User I.D. : _____

Email Used : _____

Password : _____

Password Change	Date

Notes :
_____
_____
_____
_____

Password Journal

Account Name: _____

Website : _____

User I.D. : _____

Email Used : _____

Password : _____

Password Change	Date

Notes :
_____
_____
_____
_____

Account Name: _____

Website : _____

User I.D. : _____

Email Used : _____

Password : _____

Password Change	Date

Notes :
_____
_____
_____
_____

Account Name: _____

Website : _____

User I.D. : _____

Email Used : _____

Password : _____

Password Change	Date

Notes :
_____
_____
_____

Password Journal

Account Name: _____

Website : _____

User I.D. : _____

Email Used : _____

Password : _____

Password Change	Date

Notes :
_____
_____
_____
_____

i ♥ Purple

Account Name: _____

Website : _____

User I.D. : _____

Email Used : _____

Password : _____

Password Change	Date

Notes :
_____
_____
_____

Account Name: _____

Website : _____

User I.D. : _____

Email Used : _____

Password : _____

Password Change	Date

i ♥ Purple

Notes :
_____
_____
_____

Password Journal

Account Name: _____

Website : _____

User I.D. : _____

Email Used : _____

Password : _____

Password Change	Date

Notes :
_____
_____
_____
_____

Account Name: _____

Website : _____

User I.D. : _____

Email Used : _____

Password : _____

Password Change	Date

Notes :
_____
_____
_____
_____

Account Name: _____

Website : _____

User I.D. : _____

Email Used : _____

Password : _____

Password Change	Date

Notes :
_____
_____
_____

Password Journal

Account Name: _____

Website : _____

User I.D. : _____

Email Used : _____

Password : _____

Password Change	Date

Notes :
_____
_____
_____
_____

i 🖤 Purple

Account Name: _____

Website : _____

User I.D. : _____

Email Used : _____

Password : _____

Password Change	Date

Notes :
_____
_____
_____
_____

Account Name: _____

Website : _____

User I.D. : _____

Email Used : _____

Password : _____

Password Change	Date

i 🖤 Purple

Notes :
_____
_____
_____
_____

Password Journal

Notes

Password Journal

Account Name: _____

Website : _____

User I.D. : _____

Email Used : _____

Password : _____

Password Change	Date

Notes :
_____
_____
_____
_____

Notes :
_____
_____
_____
_____

Account Name: _____

Website : _____

User I.D. : _____

Email Used : _____

Password : _____

Password Change	Date

Account Name: _____

Website : _____

User I.D. : _____

Email Used : _____

Password : _____

Password Change	Date

Notes :
_____
_____
_____

Password Journal

Account Name: _____

Website : _____

User I.D. : _____

Email Used : _____

Password : _____

Password Change	Date

Notes :
_____
_____
_____
_____

Account Name: _____

Website : _____

User I.D. : _____

Email Used : _____

Password : _____

Password Change	Date

Notes :
_____
_____
_____
_____

Account Name: _____

Website : _____

User I.D. : _____

Email Used : _____

Password : _____

Password Change	Date

Notes :
_____
_____
_____

Password Journal

Account Name: _____

Website : _____

User I.D. : _____

Email Used : _____

Password : _____

Password Change	Date

Notes : _____
_____
_____
_____
_____

Account Name: _____

Website : _____

User I.D. : _____

Email Used : _____

Password : _____

Password Change	Date

Notes : _____
_____
_____
_____

Account Name: _____

Website : _____

User I.D. : _____

Email Used : _____

Password : _____

Password Change	Date

Notes : _____
_____
_____

Password Journal

Account Name: _____

Website : _____

User I.D. : _____

Email Used : _____

Password : _____

Password Change	Date

Notes :

_____
_____
_____
_____

Account Name: _____

Website : _____

User I.D. : _____

Email Used : _____

Password : _____

Password Change	Date

Notes :

_____
_____
_____
_____

Account Name: _____

Website : _____

User I.D. : _____

Email Used : _____

Password : _____

Password Change	Date

Notes :

_____
_____
_____
_____

Password Journal

Account Name: _____

Website : _____

User I.D. : _____

Email Used : _____

Password : _____

Password Change	Date

Notes :
_____
_____
_____
_____

i ♥ purple

Account Name: _____

Website : _____

User I.D. : _____

Email Used : _____

Password : _____

Password Change	Date

Notes :
_____
_____
_____
_____

Account Name: _____

Website : _____

User I.D. : _____

Email Used : _____

Password : _____

Password Change	Date

i ♥ purple

Notes :
_____
_____
_____
_____

Password Journal

Notes

Notes

www.ingramcontent.com/pod-product-compliance
Lightning Source LLC
Chambersburg PA
CBHW081334090426
42737CB00017B/3143